Bulldogs

Dog Books for Kids

By
K. Bennett

Mendon Cottage Books

JD-Biz Publishing

Read More Amazing Animal Books

Purchase at Amazon.com

Bulldogs

Table of Contents

Introduction

Author Bio

Introduction

Dogs are not our whole life, but they make our lives whole.
~ Roger Caras

Bulldogs are heavy set dogs with lots of muscles and a wrinkly face. They have a wide head and shoulders, lots of hanging skin, pointy teeth and droopy eyes.

Their coat is shiny and short with varied colors like brindle, red, fawn and white. This breed can weigh between 45- 55 pounds. And a full grown female is about 45 pounds.

The name of the dog might make you think isn't too friendly. But the American Kennel Club says the bulldog's behavior should be: *"equable and kind, resolute, and courageous (not vicious or aggressive), and demeanor should be pacific and dignified..."*

So this breed is known as patient, friendly and kind in nature. But these qualities are not by accident.

Over the years a lot of work has been done to turn the bulldog into a friendlier pet. Today, it is usually well behaved and has a loving nature.

It gets along well with other pets and other dogs. It can also become so attached to its owner that it won't move without them. And when it comes to affection the bulldog is hard to beat. They would prefer to snuggle next to you than chase a ball around the yard.

This is one reason why they are called: ***Couch potatoes***!

Bulldogs are known to drool and slobber all over you. They snore when they sleep, they can snort often and they grunt even more. And when they walk, they shuffle from place to place. Add a little bit of gas (often smelly) into the mix, and you have quite an interesting pet in your family home!

They also have a hard time with commands. To put it simply: They are stubborn as a bull…dog! But don't worry. There is no doubt their clownish behavior, goofy antics, crazy faces and courageous nature will bring a smile to your face, and a warm feeling to your heart.

For these reasons and more, Bulldogs are recommended as a loving companion, well deserving of the title… *man's best friend*!

How about a bath?

# Chapter 1

An interesting start – England

The Bulldogs we know today originated from England. And the original name for Bulldogs was written differently in those days. But in the year 1631 – 1632, a letter was sent by a man named Preswick Eaton requesting "two good bulldogs," to be sent by ship. So the name we know today started many years ago.

Sadly, the reason the breed was known as Bulldogs is because of a sport called *bull baiting*. To put it simply, it was a contest between the bull and the dog. Many times this contest did not end well for either the bull or the dog.

As time went on and due to this sport, dogs developed muscular bodies and aggressive behavior. It is not surprising to hear this. If you had to constantly fight to live, you might get a little aggressive too!

Thankfully, in the year 1835 the '*Cruelty to Animals act*' put an end to this practice. This led to protection for the animals and this included Bulldogs. After this declaration and as years went by, the English Bulldogs were no longer useful to many people. But the emigrants saw things differently. How so?

Around the middle of the 17th century in the city of New York, Bulldogs were used by Richard Nicolls. He was the governor during those days. He decided Bulldogs could be used to corner and lead bulls. So the dogs were trained to help workers catch a bull by the nose, and hold it long enough to get a rope around its neck.

Then a man by the name of Bill George started to promote the idea of Bulldogs as pets. And the rest is history as they say!

In the year 1886, Bulldogs were officially recognized by the AKC.

To think about: Bulldogs can have serious health problems, and their lifespan is not like other breeds. Before you get this lovable pet, some research may be needed to ensure your pet enjoys the best and longest life possible.

Note of advice: Bulldogs like other breeds thrive on a close relationship. That means you are an inseparable part of the Bulldog's life. If you leave your pet alone for long periods of time, they may get upset. This leads to lots of chewing sprees that can tear up your furniture, leaving bits and pieces all over your home! So some level of responsibility is required to ensure a happy pet and a stable home.

A little walk with work...but not too much!

Bring on the love...

Dogtime.com calls the bulldog a 'lover not a fighter!' And this statement is the essence of a Bulldogs character. They are friendly and eager to get along, especially with young ones.

There is a level of curiosity in this breed and a playful nature. This means when it comes to a family with children, Bulldogs are an ideal pet. There is some level of socialization required when the introduction is made, but once the love is there, you are good to go!

Terrifcpets.com notes that '*one of the reasons the Bulldog stands out as great with children is their tolerance and patience.*'

They are happy to play with little ones and can keep going for a very long time. Sometimes they have so much fun they may not understand when enough is enough. And if the Bulldog gets tired of being tormented by little ones, he / she will walk away and find a nice spot to relax! So this pet is wonderful for a home with small children.

Bulldogs also get along great with other pets, especially those smaller than they are. Again a level of socialization is needed, but with a little time and patience all of your pets will get along just fine.

Despite their tolerance to spend time with children, Bulldogs are laid back and content to lead a simple life. They would much prefer to relax and watch your moves with an adoring gaze.

This relaxed attitude does not mean they don't need something to do. Remember this particular breed loves to chew! So it would be great to have an assortment of toys or objects for your dog to slobber over.

Although they are not great watchdogs, a Bulldog will defend the family if needed. So this makes them great guardians. And even though they don't bark a lot, if they have something to say, they will say it!

Quite a unique personality, don't you think?

Important note: Bulldogs have a lot of fun playing with children but because of the shape of their head and body, they can get overheated and suffer from heatstroke!

The best way to solve this issue is have your dog take a break between playtimes, to keep their body temperature down. This will avoid the danger of overheating and will ensure your pet stays healthy.

Shhhh....taking a break

🐾 Chapter 2

Now that you know what Bulldogs are like and their origins, let us briefly review its features:

In review: Bulldogs are loyal dogs with a patient and loving heart. They may look aggressive and dangerous, but nothing could be further from the truth.

They thrive in a close knit relationship, and love being with you. Most of the times they may not act like a pet, but more like a member of the family.

As a couch-potato, Bulldogs love a tranquil, laid back life. They prefer a relaxed atmosphere instead of runarounds. This does not mean they don't need exercise, but they are not an active type of dog.

They are even friendly with other animals (cats, dogs, etc) once they are properly socialized.

However, when it comes to training, a Bulldog is not the ideal pet to teach. But once they understand what is needed, you will not have to teach them again!

Would you like to get one?

A quick word of advice: It is important to take your Bulldog for walks on a daily basis, despite their laid back nature. Why? Well, they have a tendency to get a little overweight, so the right exercise will keep them in good shape.

FUN FACTS **FOR KIDS**: Do you know when the name Bulldog first appeared? It was around the 1500's and the the name was spelled differently than today. To give you a hint, it is a word with **8 letters** and ends with the letters: gge. Another way to spell the name is a word with **9 letters** and also ends with the letters: gge. Can you guess the words? Ask your parents or a guardian to help you search!

Nice and clean

- *How much can they weigh?* The male can weigh approximately 45-55 pounds. The female can weigh approximately 40-45 pounds. This doesn't mean a Bulldog can't weigh more / less than this, but this is the standard weight.

-*How tall can they get?* Bulldogs can reach 12 - 16 inches in height.

-*What about babies?* The female can have between 4-5 puppies. A Caesarean delivery is needed for many births because of the size of the head.

-*How long to they live?* Lifespan is usually between 7-12 years.

-*What about their coat?* Bulldogs have a short, beautiful, shiny coat.

-*How often do they shed?* Bulldogs do shed so you may need to brush your pet often. If you suffer from allergies, this is something to think about.

-*What color are they?* Bulldogs have beautiful coats in lustrous shades of brindle, piebald, white, red, light brown and fawn.

- *What about their temperament or personality?* As noted previously, Bulldogs have a patient and gentle nature. But they can be bullheaded and stubborn. But don't worry! This part of their personality will not affect their love and constant devotion to you.

A moment of peace and tranquility

Caring for your Bulldog

Bulldogs are not only our pets, but also valued members of our home. So we want to be sure they get proper care and like most, if not all of us, the right diet and exercise is important.

Feeding your pet will depend on factors like size, build, metabolism, etc. Where a Bulldog is concerned food is something we need to watch. Why? A Bulldog can overeat and too much weight will affect their health.

We want to ensure our pet gets the best nutrition possible, so we need to think about the portion of food we are feeding them and what kind of food (preferably nutritious) it is.

For example, **Dogtime.com** recommends the following portions of food:

Half to two cups of food per day divided into two meals. This food should be good, nutritious meals to help your dog have a healthy diet.

This means food should be put away after your pet eats. Why? If you leave food around so your pet can eat whenever he / she feels like it, you may have a problem later on.

A snack right now would be good :-)

Mealtime

There are lots of choices to feed your Bulldog, so it may be hard to choose the best food on the market. These steps (below) will help you make an informed and honest decision regarding the best dog food for your beloved pet. (This advice applies to other breeds as well).

Grrmf.org notes the following recommendations to ensure a happy and well fed pet.

Scratch chemical preservatives: Be on the lookout for ingredients like Ethoxyquin, BHT, BHA, propelyne glycol or sodium nitrates in any form. That includes sodium nitrites too! Instead look for natural preservatives such as Rosemary (herbs), and natural Tocopherols.

Expiration date: Be sure to check the expiration date on the bag. You should purchase food months ahead of this date. Why? Moldy food could be a health factor and you never want to feed your dog this kind of food, which can affect its good health. Usually the bag itself is an indicator. Does it look fresh or do you see grease stains somewhere? Stay away from those unsavory looking bags! Ask the store helpers if you are not sure whether the bag is fresh or not.

A bite of meat: Meat ingredient is a great choice, but be sure it is the FIRST ingredient. This can be Turkey, Lamb or Chicken. Do not buy food with Grain as the first ingredient. Why not? Meat protein is what you are looking for. This is the best nutrition for your pet so search for the meat ingredient as one of the most (if not the most) important in the list. Remember your pet needs animal protein for a beneficial diet.

Avoid animal digest: This is the intestines of other animals! They can contain feet, heads and slaughterhouse waste of other animals. An example as noted at the website is "poultry byproducts."

Sugars and artificial colors: These additives are not healthy or beneficial for your pet so avoid them.

Dog treats: Try to get healthy treats! There are many out there with ingredients that could harm your pet. You could try your hand at making them yourself. Make it family project and have some fun.

The list could go on and on, but you get the idea! Of course if you have the time to make home cooked food for your pet it would be a great alternative to ensure healthy meals.

The website **Bulldogpros.com** noted some great tips to help give the best nutrition to your pet.

The most important ingredients to remember are:

-Proteins from meat

-Fiber (Just like us, your pet needs generous helpings of fiber to keep their digestive track in the best condition possible)

-Omega 3 and 6 (This will help you pet's skin and coat to keep a healthy glow!)

<u>Caution:</u> We all know what foods **<u>NOT</u>** to feed our dogs. You may instantly think of chocolate. But you can add to this list: mushrooms, caffeine, onions, fruit seeds, grapes, raisins and more. If you are unsure of the entire list, look online to see what other foods you need to avoid. And if you are underage, please consult with a parent or guardian before you start your search.

Taking a break

<u>Important to know:</u> Bulldogs can get very sick and and can be affected by some conditions. They have a number of things that may affect them during their lifetime like: *Head shakes, cherry eye, reverse sneezing, hip and tail problems* and more. This may not apply to your pet, but it is important to know just in case. Your veterinarian can help you with the best care and suggestions for a healthy and happy pet.

Exercises

Although Bulldogs are laid back and relaxed, the right exercise will keep your pet active and in good health.

-Walking

Walking is a great way to give your pet the exercise they need!

-Soft run

One of the best ways to keep your Bulldog happy is by stretching their legs into a soft run. (Not too fast…remember Bulldogs cannot get too overheated) And try to stay away from really hard surfaces. An open field (park area or similar site) is better for its low impact on the frame of your pet. This will help their joints and feet to keep in tip top shape.

- Indoor activities

Bulldogs love being indoors so you can take this opportunity to develop fun activities. This is a great help for their exercise routine. And you will not have to expend a great deal of energy outdoors to ensure your pet gets adequate exercise.

- Swimming

This is another great way to exercise your pet, but you must be careful. Bulldogs are not great swimmers and can drown easily. If you take your pet to the water, watch them carefully so they don't get too tired!

-Socializing

(If you see someone with a dog, don't fly by! Stop for a moment and help your dog to know it is all right to meet others. Don't forget the importance of socialization for a well-rounded pet.)

Making friends

The Right Training

Training a Bulldog is not for the faint of heart. So how will you handle it? One way is by the following:

Keeping it effective

Michele Welton from the website *'your pure bred puppy'* recommends the following training method. (This applies to all dog breeds and not just Bulldogs, but with Bulldogs this is a nice way to try to get them to follow your commands.)

Try: RESPECT TRAINING.

This is where you actually teach your pet to learn from POSITIVE and NEGATIVE consequences.

As a human we also learn from these same principles. For example: If we do something for someone and they say thank you, we may do it again. And yet if we forget to take out the garbage, and Daddy blows his top, more than likely we will not do it again. (At least we hope!)

Dogs, and in this case Bulldogs, learn in the same way. If our pet does something great we can reward it with smiles, hugs, laughs, kisses, games, treats, and whatever other happy outcome you will like. Trust me when I say Bulldogs will LOVE it! They will simply slobber all over you to show how they really care for you.

Of course, if our pet does something we do not like we can transmit that with our voice, our look or use the leash or collar. It is important to note you will not hit, kick or otherwise abuse the animal. A simple tug with a firm voice is usually enough for the animal to figure out something is off.

This dignifies the dog and teaches it both respect and appreciation for boundaries. With loving attention and care, you can have a happy, obedient pet and a happy home.

If you are unsure how to do this or if you feel overwhelmed with the task, talk to a reputable veterinarian. You can also look up the training methods or obedience lessons online.

*** There are many other good methods to try, but this will give you a stepping stone to get started!*

🐾 Chapter 3

Nice and cool!

So, what else can we learn about Bulldogs? Check out some other interesting details you may like to know.

- This breed is the most famous for being delivered by caesarean because their head is a little big. So, approximately 80 % of the births are done this way. If you do not understand what a caesarean birth is, ask your parents to explain it to you.

- This dog is not a very good swimmer because of their large frame, particularly their head. So keep them away from the water because they can drown if not careful.

- Bulldogs are very popular mascots, and have even won awards. On the TV show "Modern Family," Stella (French bulldog) is the first to have won the Golden Collar Award for "Best dog in a scripted series". Way to go Stella!

- Bulldogs are mascots for many schools and very popular too! Around 40 universities in the United States have sports teams named after this wonderful breed. This does not include smaller schools and colleges, so this breed is not only well known, but well-loved too.

-The hood ornament for Mack Trucks is none other than...a Bulldog!

-Bulldogs are good at...skating! Don't take my word for it. Look up the names of Bazooka, Tillman, Vegas, Chief and more. Or do a quick Google search with the phrase: *Bulldog skateboarding.* Amazing!

Out for a stroll

FUN FACTS FOR KIDS: Do you know which US president had an English Bulldog at the White House? It would be the 29th president. Ask your parents or a guardian for permission to search online to find out the name of the dog!

Conclusion

Bonding time

In conclusion:

Bulldogs are beautiful couch potatoes and a great family pet. Yes, they can be stubborn, independent and bull headed, but their heart is just as big as their head!

This beautiful breed is more of a family member than a pet, and they act that way. They love being underfoot basking in your loving attention. Your happiness is their happiness, and they will not hesitate to show it with slobbering kisses and drooling nudges.

They love children and enjoy playing with them. Although a Bulldog's lifespan is not as long as other breeds, their goofy and clownish behavior will bring a smile to your heart and leave you wanting for more.

If you decide to make this gentle breed a part of your home, you could not make a better choice than an affectionate and dependable pet!

Author Bio

K. Bennett is a native from the Island of Roatan, North of Honduras. She loves to write about many different subjects, but writing for children is special to her heart.

Some of her favorite pastimes are reading, traveling and discovering new things. These activities help to fuel her imagination and act like a canvas for more stories.

She also loves fantasy elements like hidden worlds and faraway lands. Basically anything that gets her imagination soaring to new heights!

Her writing credits include children books online, short stories for online magazines, and two novellas listed at Amazon.com

Our books are available at

1. Amazon.com

2. Barnes and Noble

3. Itunes

4. Kobo

5. Smashwords

6. Google Play Books

This book is published by

JD-Biz Corp

P O Box 374

Mendon, Utah 84325

http://www.jd-biz.com/

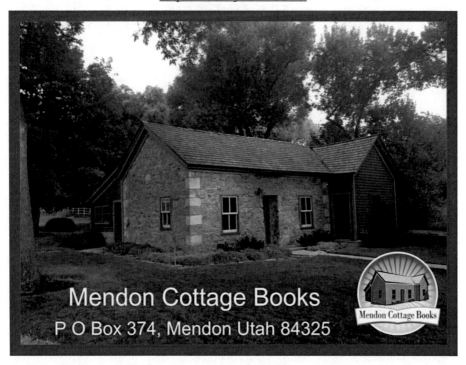

Top Ten Dog Breeds For Kids

Amazing Animal Books
For Young Readers

Kisha Bennett & John Davidson

Poodles

Dog Books for Kids

K. Bennett

Labrador Retrievers

Dog Books for Kids

K. Bennett

German Shepherds

Dog Books for Kids

K. Bennett

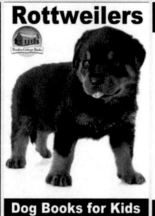

Rottweilers

Dog Books for Kids

K. Bennett

Boxers

Dog Books for Kids

K. Bennett

Golden Retrievers

Dog Books for Kids

K. Bennett

Beagles

Dog Books for Kids

K. Bennett

Yorkies

Dog Books for Kids

K. Bennett

Bulldogs

Horses
For Kids
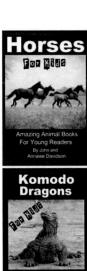
Amazing Animal Books
For Young Readers
By John and
Annalee Davidson

Wolves
For Kids

Amazing Animal Books
For Young Readers
By John Davidson and Virginia Fidler

Lady Bugs
For Kids
Amazing Animal Books
For Young Readers
By Jean Hall & John Davidson

Sasquatch - Yeti
Abominable Snowman
Bigfoot
For Kids

Amazing Animal Books
For Young Readers
By John Davidson

Penguins
For Kids

Amazing Animal Books
For Young Readers
Kim Chase & John Davidson

Komodo
Dragons
For Kids
Amazing Animal Books
For Young Readers
By Lisa Barry & John Davidson

Cats
For Kids
Amazing Animal Books
For Young Readers
K. Bennett & John Davidson

Spiders
For Kids
Amazing Animal Books
For Young Readers
By John Davidson

Giant Panda
Bears
For Kids

Amazing Animal Books
For Young Readers
By John Davidson

Animals of
North America
For Kids

Amazing Animal Books
For Young Readers
By John Davidson

Birds of
North America
For Kids
Amazing Animal Books
For Young Readers
By John Davidson

Dolphins
For Kids

Amazing Animal Books
For Young Readers
By John Davidson and Natalia Asfar

Hamsters
For Kids

Amazing Animal Books
For Young Readers
John Davidson

Polar Bears
For Kids

Amazing Animal Books
For Young Readers
By John Davidson and Kim Chase

Turtles
For Kids

Amazing Animal Books
For Young Readers
By John Davidson and Natalia Asfar

Walruses
For Kids

Amazing Animal Books
For Young Readers
By John Davidson and Kim Chase

My First Book About
Animals of
Australia

Amazing Animal Books
By Annalee and John Davidson
Children's Picture Books

Goats
For Kids

Amazing Animal Books
For Young Readers
Rachel Smith & John Davidson

Flamingos
For Kids

Amazing Animal Books
For Young Readers
K. Bennett & John Davidson

Giraffes
For Kids

Amazing Animal Books
For Young Readers
Valeria Arcas & John Davidson

Eagles

For Kids
Amazing Animal Books
For Young Readers
Nicholas Williams & John Davidson

Bears
For Kids

Amazing Animal Books
For Young Readers
Zahra Jazeel & John Davidson

Parrots
For Kids

Amazing Animal Books
For Young Readers
Zahra Jazeel & John Davidson

My First Book About
Kittens
Amazing Animal Books
By John Davidson
Children's Picture Books

Sharks
For Kids

Amazing Animal Books
For Young Readers
By John Davidson

Bulldogs

Bulldogs

47660518R00018

Made in the USA
San Bernardino, CA
05 April 2017